W9-CQO-598

420 Ways to Clean Everything

by Harriet Wylie

Bonanza Books/New York

To my mother and father

This 1989 edition is published by Bonanza Books, distributed
by Crown Publishers, Inc.,225 Park Avenue South, New York,
New York 10003, by arrangement with Harmony Books, a
division of Crown Publishers, Inc.

Manufactured in the United States of America

Library of Congress Cataloging-in-Publication Data

Wylie, Harriet.
    420 ways to clean everything / by Harriet Wylie.—1989 ed.
    Reprint. Originally published: New York : Harmony Books,
1980.
    Includes index.
    ISBN 0-517-67694-X
    1. Cleaning.   I. Title.   II. Title: Four hundred twenty ways
to clean everything.
TX324.W94   1989
648—dc19   88-39789
                                                      CIP

h g f e d c

Contents

Introduction

I began collecting recipes for this book after a casual inquiry from a friend on how to clean ivory beads. While finding out, I came across so many other tips that I began to take a more serious interest in the whole business of cleaning. Old recipes and books came flooding in from relatives and friends and it became as big a job deciding what should be left out as choosing what should go in.

Most of the recipes are from old books, some as far back as 1810, but alas a number of the marvelous early formulas had to be omitted as they contain chemicals that are either no longer available or are highly dangerous. As far as I can tell, all the ingredients in this book are readily available from pharmacists, grocers, hardware stores, builders' merchants or art suppliers.

All ingredients marked with an asterisk* are poisonous, inflammable, caustic or toxic and must be used with care. Precautions can be found for each chemical in the Glossary.

I hope you will have fun trying some of these interesting alternatives to modern products and discovering that they really work just as well.

Carpets
Carpets
Carpets
Carpets
Carpets
Carpets
Carpets
Carpets

Angora Rugs

See Furs under "Fabrics" (page 63).

Brighten Faded Carpets

Remove dust with a vacuum cleaner. Then mix together 1 qt. (1 liter) white vinegar and 3 qts. (3 liters) boiling water. Wipe the carpet with the mixture, keeping the cloth fairly dry to prevent saturating the backing, then dry thoroughly and air well. Then rub the surface with warm bread crumbs to revive the color and vacuum.

Carpet Soap

Dissolve ¼ cup (60 grams) yellow soap in 1 qt. (1 liter) boiling water, then add 1 tablespoon (15 grams) washing soda and 3 tablespoons *ammonia. Mix together and pour into jars.

Mix 2 tablespoons of the mixture to 1 qt. (1 liter) warm water and apply to the carpet with a brush or flannel cloth. Rub hard and rinse off with a clean cloth and water. Dry well with a cloth and air thoroughly. Do not saturate the carpet with water as it will rot the backing.

Creeping Rugs

To prevent rugs from creeping on carpets, sew a large mesh fishnet to the underside of the rug.

Curling Corners of Rugs

To prevent the corners of carpets from curling, sew a triangular canvas pocket on the underside of each corner about two inches from the edges. Then place a triangular piece of sheet lead, which can be bought from a plumber, into each pocket.

Persian and Turkish Rugs

These are sturdy, hard-wearing rugs that will withstand heavy usage if cared for properly.

Remove all dust frequently with a vacuum cleaner. Always sweep in the direction of the pile to prevent grit and dirt from getting to the foundation of the rug and damaging the knotting.

If the rug is very dirty, wash it with carpet soap (above) and very soft water. The best soft water is obtained from a wooden rainwater bucket or barrel. Before tackling the rug, test the soap and water out on an unimportant area first to see if the colors run.

If the colors are fast and washing is suitable, clean the rug with a sponge wrung out in the water and dab on the soap. Clean only a small area at a time, starting in one corner. Rinse this area with clean water and pat dry. Repeat this until the whole rug is clean, then dry and air thoroughly. If the colors do run, abandon the soap-and-water method and sponge with *denatured alcohol or rubbing alcohol. Test on a hidden area first.

When possible, drag Oriental rugs over newly fallen snow, first on one side, then the other. Shake well and replace. This cleans the rugs and freshens the colors.

Dry-clean Turkish and Persian rugs with caution as the chemicals can ruin the wool and badly affect the colors.

For bad stains and repairs, consult an expert.

Sliding Rugs

To prevent rugs from sliding on polished floors, sew a small rectangle of thin rubber on the underside of each corner. A piece of an old hot-water bottle is ideal.

Storing Rugs

Always roll the rugs with the pile to the inside. Never fold them. Where possible, store rugs in mothproof containers.

Protect valuable rugs by backing them with felt.

Synthetic Carpets

To clean, follow the manufacturer's instructions carefully. If using chemicals, always test first.

CARPET STAINS

Alcohol

Sponge the stain with clear, warm water as soon as possible, and dry thoroughly.

Blood

Sponge the stain with cold water and pat dry with a towel. Repeat until the stain fades. Treat as soon as possible. Never use salt water on carpets as it will rot the backing.

Chocolate

To remove hard chocolate trodden into carpets, scrape off the thick pieces with a blunt knife and gently rub any remaining stain with *carbon tetrachloride.

Blot up liquid chocolate, then sponge lightly with club soda. Then sponge with clean warm water and dry thoroughly.

Cigarette Burns

Rub the mark with fine sandpaper to remove the charred fibers. Then make a mild detergent solution and drip it slowly onto the stain, and rub gently with a clean cloth. Leave for five minutes, then sponge it off with a solution made of 2 tablespoons (30 grams) borax to 2 cups (½ liter) water. Repeat if necessary, then rinse with clean water and dry well. Or scrape the stain with a silver coin to remove the singed fibers.

Grease

Cover the stain with bicarbonate of soda and rub it lightly

Note: Metric equivalents have been rounded off for convenience.

into the pile. Leave for one hour to absorb the grease, then brush off carefully with a clean brush. Repeat if necessary.

Wipe persistent stains with *carbon tetrachloride, but test in an unimportant area first.

To remove dust and grease spots from carpets, vacuum-clean well, then mix 1 teaspoon *ammonia and ¾ cup *turpentine into a bucket of warm water. Wipe the carpet with the mixture, keeping the cloth fairly dry. Rinse with clean water and dry thoroughly.

Ink

Spread cream of tartar on the stain and squeeze a few drops of lemon juice onto the powder. Then rub into the stain with a clean cloth and leave for only a minute. Brush off the powder with a clean brush and sponge immediately with warm water. Repeat if necessary, but do not leave the lemon juice on for more than one minute.

If the stains are fresh, cover with a layer of fuller's earth mixed into a paste with water, and leave to dry. Then brush off and repeat if necessary.

Or rub the stain with sour milk and leave for a few minutes, then wipe off with a clean dry cloth. Then rub with warm water and a few drops of *ammonia.

Ink (Ballpoint)

Sponge the stain with *denatured alcohol. Drip the solvent onto the stain and, when the ink has dissolved, rub with a clean cloth and more alcohol.

Care must be taken with synthetic fibers as the alcohol can dissolve them, so always test an unimportant area.

Milk, Milky Tea and Coffee

To remove the grease, drip a mild detergent solution or *carbon tetrachloride onto the stain, then sponge off with warm water and dry well.

Rainwater

Sponge the stain with a cloth dipped in *denatured alcohol. Repeat until the stain fades.

Rust

Add 1 teaspoon each cream of tartar and lemon juice to 2 cups (½ liter) water and sponge onto the stain and leave for one minute. Rinse off with clean water quickly and dry well.

Soot

To remove soot from carpets, cover the stain with a thick layer of salt, and carefully sweep it up. Never wet the soot as it will only make the stain worse.

Tea and Coffee

Blot up the excess quickly and sponge with warm water, then dry well. This process should be enough if there is no milk in the tea or coffee. (See Milk, above.)

Urine

Mop up the excess with tissues or an old rag, then sponge well with clean, warm water and rub dry. Repeat, taking care not to saturate the backing fiber. Make a solution of 3 tablespoons white vinegar and 1 teaspoon liquid detergent. Mix together well, drip it slowly onto the stain, and leave for fifteen minutes. Then rinse off with clean water and rub dry.

Water

Flooding and leaks must be dealt with immediately. Mop up the excess quickly, and prop a stool or box under the wet area. Place a fan near it to circulate the air and dry it as quickly as possible. This is only suitable if the damp area is relatively small, but if the flooding is extensive, dry the carpet in the open air.

Once the carpet is dry, stains can be removed by dripping a mild detergent solution onto the area. Wipe off with a clean cloth, then rinse and dry thoroughly.

Consult an expert if the stains are severe.

Wine

Soak up the excess as soon as possible and sprinkle the stain with an absorbent powder. Salt, fuller's earth, powdered borax and talcum powder are all suitable. When the powder becomes sticky, carefully remove and add more clean powder.

Repeat until most of the stain has gone, then apply a final layer of powder and leave for two hours. Finally brush it off. Remove the remaining stain with a mild detergent solution and rinse quickly with clean water. Rub dry and air well.

Floors
Floors
Floors
Floors
Floors
Floors
Floors

Coconut Matting

To clean coconut matting, beat it well to remove the dust. Then scrub it with warm salt water on both sides. If it is very dirty, use soap as well as the salt-water method. In both cases rinse well with warm, then cold water. Then hang outside to dry, keeping the matting as flat as possible. Do not hang it over a clothesline as this will leave a permanent crease in it.

Economical Floor Polishes

Empty half a new can of floor polish into another can and fill up both the cans with *kerosene. Place the cans in a pan of cold water and bring to the boil, to melt the polish. Stir well, then cool. This diluted polish is just as effective as new polish.

Save all old ends of burned candles. When a good quantity has been collected, shred them into a pan and measure the contents. Remove any wicks, and add an equal quantity of *turpentine to the wax. Place the pan into another pan of cold water and bring to the boil, to melt the wax. Stir well, then pour the mixture into cans and cool. Warm the polish slightly before use to make polishing easier.

Economical Polish

Mix together 1 cup (¼ liter) *kerosene and 1 cup (¼ liter) white vinegar in a bottle and shake well before use. Use for cleaning tiles, linoleum, marble and baseboards.

Floor and Wall Tiles

Dissolve ½ cup (115 grams) shredded coarse soap and ½ cup (115 grams) washing soda in 1 gallon (4 liters) hot water. Using a stiff brush, scrub the tiles with the mixture, then rinse and dry.

To remove cement from floor tiles, rub well with a little linseed oil on a cloth.

Rub glazed tiles with a cut lemon and leave for fifteen minutes, then polish with a soft cloth.

To clean discolored tiles, wash with hot water and a little *kerosene.

Rub the tiles with tailor's chalk and a damp cloth to remove brown stains.

Mix equal parts of linseed oil and *turpentine to polish the tiles. This will prevent the glaze from cracking and will also produce a good sheen.

Linoleum

To clean linoleum, wipe it with a clean cloth wrung out in lukewarm water, and dry well. Then rub with a cloth dipped in a little warmed linseed oil to produce a good sheen.

To freshen old linoleum, mix 1 qt. (1 liter) fresh milk with 1 qt. (1 liter) *turpentine. Rub the mixture onto the floor and polish with a warmed soft cloth.

Never use soap, *ammonia or soap powders on linoleum as they cause the surface to crack and the color to fade.

Polish for Parquet Floors

Dissolve ¼ cup (60 grams) beeswax in 1 cup (¼ liter) *turpentine in a double pan, to make an oily mixture. Coat the floor with linseed oil, then rub on the mixture. Leave for twenty-four hours, then polish hard.

Scrubbing Mixture for Floorboards and Kitchen Tables

Mix together 1 lb. (450 grams) soft soap (see page 59), 1 lb. (450 grams) fuller's earth, 1 lb. (450 grams) washing soda, and 2 qts. (2 liters) water in a large pan. Bring to the boil and simmer until there is only half the quantity left. Then cool and store in jars.

Apply the mixture to the boards and scrub with a stiff brush and hot water. Always scrub in the direction of the grain of the wood. Then rinse and dry.

Stone Floors and Steps

To clean weather stains off stone steps, scour with a stiff brush dipped in hot soapy water mixed with 1 tablespoon *kerosene.

To remove grease stains, pour a strong solution of washing soda and boiling water onto the steps. Then cover the stains with a paste made of fuller's earth and hot water. Leave overnight and rinse. Repeat if necessary.

To prevent steps from freezing up in winter, add an aspirin and 1 tablespoon *denatured alcohol to the final rinsing water.

Furniture
Furniture
Furniture
Furniture
Furniture
Furniture
Furniture
Furniture
Furniture
Furniture
Furniture

Acid Baths

Never use an acid bath to strip furniture as it weakens the glues and removes all the natural oils in the wood.

Bleaching

To bleach wood, scrub the surface with 1 part chlorine bleach to 10 parts water to remove the color, then rinse thoroughly with water and dry quickly with a soft rag. The wood must be sealed after this process. Mix up a thin solution of plaster of Paris and water, and apply it to the whole surface and leave to dry. Then wipe off the excess with a damp cloth. The plaster of Paris will sink into the wood and seal it below the surface. Select an alcohol-based wood stain and brush it on to the surface evenly, then brush on a coat of white oil and polish frequently and thoroughly with beeswax polish. All stages of this process are essential to prevent warping.

Brown Wicker

Scrub well with cold salty water and rinse in cold water and dry in the sun. When dry, brush with *kerosene and polish with a soft cloth.

Cane

Treat cane in the same way as rush. When dry, polish with furniture cream.

Deck Chairs

Remove the canvas and wash it in soapy water with a little *ammonia. Scrub if necessary. Rinse well and dry in the open air, then press with a warm iron. Scrub the frame and replace the canvas.

Dents

Cover dents in wood with wet blotting paper, and press with a hot iron, repeating if necessary. The compressed wood fibers will swell to their original size. Afterward polish as usual.

Dust Pump

Use a bicycle pump or hair dryer to blow away dust on bedsprings or any intricately decorated objects.

Furniture Cream for Polished Wood

Shred ½ cup (115 grams) beeswax and 2 tablespoons (30 grams) white candle wax into a pan and add 1 cup (¼ liter) *turpentine. Place the pan in another pan of boiling water and heat until the wax melts, then stir thoroughly. Then dissolve 1 tablespoon (15 grams) shredded castile soap or pure soap flakes in ½ cup (115 grams) boiling water and mix into a thick paste. When cool but still liquid, mix the two together and beat hard to a creamy consistency, and store in jars.

A wax-polished surface keeps moisture out, but it also seals it in and often prevents excessive drying which causes cracking and warping.

Furniture Polish

Shred ½ cup (115 grams) beeswax into an old pan and add 1 cup (¼ liter) *turpentine. Place the pan in another pan of boiling water and heat until the wax melts. Stir thoroughly and store in jars or cans.

Liquid Polish for Carved Wood

Mix 2 cups (½ liter) boiled linseed oil with 1 cup (¼ liter) each of the following: *denatured alcohol, *turpentine and white vinegar. Store in firmly corked bottles and shake well before use.

Picture Frames

To clean gilt frames, mix 1 egg white with 1 teaspoon bicarbonate of soda and sponge the surface with the mixture.

Or, wipe the surface with liquid detergent, then polish with a soft cloth.

To clean wooden frames, first dust, then rub with a little boiled linseed oil on a soft cloth.

Polishing Hint

To make large flat surfaces easier to polish, heat a brick or an old-fashioned flatiron in the oven until hot. Wrap the hot brick in several pieces of old blanket and apply the polish to the flat side of the blanket. Then "iron" the surface in the direction of the grain, until the whole area is covered with polish. The heat melts the wax and allows it to sink into the wood easily, and the weight of the brick eliminates arm ache.

Rush and White Wicker

To clean rush, sponge with warm salt water, then rinse with hot water and dry in the sun. If it has yellowed, sponge with lemon juice and salt, then rinse and dry. If it has sagged, clean it, then saturate with hot water and dry outside.

Saturated Wood

A safe way to dry out saturated woods is to immerse the object in *kerosene. It will slowly drive out the water, which rises to the surface. When all the water has come out, immerse the object in *gasoline to drive out the *kerosene. Then take it out, and the *gasoline will evaporate. When fully dry, polish in the usual way.

Stripping French Polished Furniture

A lot of *denatured alcohol is used in this process, so if possible work out-of-doors. If not, open all windows and doors to create a draft. The fumes are very heavy and can cause drowsiness and nausea in confined airless spaces. They are also highly inflammable, so make sure there are no naked flames nearby.

Wipe the surface with *denatured alcohol using a nylon scouring pad, in the direction of the wood grain. Use the *denatured alcohol liberally: it will dissolve the varnish and make it easy to wipe off. If the varnish is very stubborn use grade 000 steel wool. Make sure all the French polish has been removed, then wipe the surface clean with a new rag and more *denatured alcohol. Remove any stains (see pages 24–26), and apply beeswax polish with a hot brick and blankets (see page 22). Polish frequently to build up a protective sheen.

Woodworm Holes

Place the point of a penknife into the dead wormholes with the blade in the same direction as the wood grain, and push the blade in a little way to destroy the perfect circular shape of the hole. Fill the hole well with beeswax polish mixed with a wood stain to match the color of the wood. This is the best disguise for hiding the wormholes.

Woods

To clean and feed *oak*, rub the surface with boiled linseed oil on a soft cloth, then polish off the excess with a soft dry chamois cloth.

Or boil 1 qt. (1 liter) beer with 1 tablespoon (15 grams) sugar and 2 tablespoons (30 grams) beeswax, and mix thoroughly. When cool, wipe the wood with the mixture and a soft cloth. Leave to dry, then polish up with a soft dry chamois cloth.

To clean polished *mahogany*, wipe the surface with equal parts of white vinegar and warm water, then polish with a soft cloth.

To clean *walnut*, rub the surface with a little *kerosene on a soft cloth, and polish with a chamois cloth.

The above recipes for woods can be used when the furniture has a natural patina from many years of polishing and use. They can be used frequently with an occasional polishing with beeswax and *turpentine.

WOOD STAINS

Alcohol

To remove alcohol stains from wood, make a thick paste with pumice powder and boiled linseed oil, and rub the stain carefully, with the grain. Then wipe clean and rub with a little linseed oil and polish as usual.

Rub alcohol rings on wood with oil of camphor. If the stain is still wet, dab it with boiled linseed oil and leave for twelve hours. Rub hard before polishing as usual.

Candle Wax

To remove candle grease from wood, lightly scrape it with the back of a blunt knife, then polish with a chamois cloth.

Chill Marks

Cloudy "chill" marks appear on French polished furniture when exposed to extremes of temperature. To remove these marks, gently wave a lighted taper from side to side over the marks until they disappear, taking care not to scorch the varnish. Then rub over the area with a warm cloth and polish well. Keep the article in a constant temperature.

Grease and Ink

To remove grease marks and ink stains from polished wood and upholstery, mix 2 tablespoons white vinegar with 1 tablespoon water and sponge the stains in dark woods with it. Rinse well and dry, then polish as usual.

Or make up a 5% solution of *oxalic acid and apply it to the stains with a soft brush, a cork or a feather. When the stain has been removed, rinse with water and dry with clean blotting paper, then polish as usual.

Rub ink-stained white wood with half a lemon dipped in salt, then rinse well with clear water. Dry thoroughly, then polish as usual.

Hot Dish Marks

To remove hot dish marks from polished wood, simmer 2 cups (½ liter) boiled linseed oil for ten minutes and add ½ cup (115 grams) *turpentine. Apply this frequently to the stain with a soft cloth until it fades, then polish as usual.

Match Marks

Rub match marks on polished or varnished wood with half a lemon followed by a cloth dipped in warm water. Dry quickly with a cloth, then polish as usual.

Perfume

To remove perfume stains from polished wood, rub the stain lightly and quickly with a little *denatured alcohol followed by plenty of boiled linseed oil. If the stain is very obstinate, leave some oil on the surface for twenty-four hours, then wipe clean with a soft cloth and polish as usual.

Do not use *denatured alcohol on varnished surfaces as it will dissolve the varnish.

Scratches

To get rid of scratch marks on wood, mix equal parts of boiled linseed oil and *turpentine and rub it gently into the scratch. Continue to rub until the scratch fades, then polish as usual.

Water

Rub water stains on polished wood with petroleum jelly or boiled linseed oil and repeat frequently.

White Marks

Rub white stains on highly polished wood with any of the following ingredients: oil of camphor, the cut edge of a shelled Brazil nut, silver polishes (page 31), or a mixture of cigar ash and olive oil. Then polish as usual.

Polishes used on metals should not be used on woods.

UPHOLSTERY STAINS

Fabric Stains
See "Fabrics" (pages 61–76) for particular stains.

Leather Upholstery Stains
See "Leather" (pages 33–38) for leather upholstery and Morocco leather.

Upholstery Stains
Mix any of the following: tailor's chalk, talcum powder, starch or fuller's earth with water to make a thick paste, and apply it to the fabric to remove a variety of stains safely.

Remove dust and loose dirt with a vacuum cleaner.

Metals
Metals
Metals
Metals
Metals
Metals
Metals

Aluminum

To clean aluminum articles, wash with a solution of hot soapy water and a little *ammonia. Dry thoroughly and rub with dry table salt, then polish with a soft cloth.

Never use washing soda on aluminum.

Brass

To clean very dirty brass, boil the article in a pan of water with 1 tablespoon salt and 1 cup (¼ liter) white vinegar for several hours.

Wash engraved and Indian brass in soapy water and polish with a chamois cloth. If it is stained, rub with lemon juice and salt, then wash immediately in hot soapy water. Rinse, dry and polish with a chamois cloth.

Never scour lacquered or varnished brass. Apply a paste made of lemon juice and cream of tartar, and leave on for five minutes. Then wash in warm water and dry with a soft cloth.

To remove lacquer, sponge the article with *denatured alcohol. Lemon juice mixed with metal polish will help to keep the article clean longer.

Bronze

To clean bronze, dust well, then rub the surface with a little warmed linseed oil, and polish with a chamois cloth.

Chromium

Wash in warm soapy water and rinse well, then dry thoroughly. Polish with bicarbonate of soda or *denatured alcohol.

To store chromium articles for long periods of time, first dismantle if necessary and coat the entire surface with a thick layer of petroleum jelly. Make sure hinges, bolts and screws are well covered, then hang up to store. Wash off the jelly in hot soapy water and dry thoroughly before reusing.

Copper

Wash in hot soapy water and rub dry with a soft chamois cloth, then air thoroughly. To clean very dirty copper, boil the article in a pan of water with salt and white vinegar for several hours.

If tarnished, rub with a mixture of salt and white vinegar or half a lemon dipped in salt. Rinse quickly and wash in hot soapy water. Then rinse again and dry well.

If the article is caked with grime and smoke, or corroded in areas, soak in a weak solution of *ammonia and cold water and gently rub with steel wool (grade 000). Dry quickly and polish with a paste made from wood ash and *denatured alcohol.

Door Plates

When cleaning door plates, cut the exact shape and size of the door plates out of thick card. Place the template round the plate while cleaning to protect the surrounding surface.

Egg-Stained Silver

Rub salt on egg-stained silver with the fingertips, then rinse well and clean as usual.

Electroplate

Wash with warm water and a little *ammonia, and dry. Then rub with cigar ash and polish with a soft cloth.

Enamel

Scrub enamelware with washing soda and hot water, then rinse and dry. If stained, rub with lemon juice and salt, then rinse and dry.

Gold

Wash plain gold articles in lukewarm soapy water and dry with a cotton cloth, then polish vigorously with a chamois cloth.

Wash filigree gold in lukewarm water with a little *ammonia added, then dry and polish with a chamois cloth.

To clean gold and silver lace, sew the lace in a linen cloth. Place the bag in a pan of soapy water—2 cups (½ liter) water to ¼ cup (60 grams) soap—and boil for thirty minutes. With lace still in bag, rinse thoroughly, and then lay the lace out flat to dry.

Iron and Steel

If the article is in good condition, gently rub with fine emery paper and wipe with a soft cloth dipped in olive oil.

If the article is rusty, soak in *kerosene for one or two days to soften the rust, then gently rub the surface, while wet, with emery paper.

If the rust is very bad, flake it off with an old knife or chisel, then soak in *kerosene and brush briskly with a wire brush. When clean, rub with emery powder.

In all cases, when clean, dry thoroughly and seal the surface from the air with petroleum jelly or a mineral oil.

Pewter

Mix a thick paste made of cigar ash or whiting and linseed oil. Wet a cloth in a mixture of equal parts of linseed oil and *turpentine, and use this to apply the paste to the article. When clean, wash in hot soapy water, dry thoroughly and polish with a chamois cloth.

Silver Dip

Half fill a Mason jar with thin aluminum foil, then add

2 tablespoons kosher salt, and fill the jar with cold water. Cover the jar carefully and keep it near the kitchen sink. Dip stained cutlery in the mixture and leave for two minutes to remove the stains, then rinse thoroughly.

Silver Jewelry

Rub the article with toothpaste or damp tooth powder with a soft cloth. Rinse well in warm water and polish with a chamois cloth.

Silver Polishes

Dissolve 2 tablespoons (30 grams) powdered alum and ½ cup (115 grams) talcum powder in 1 cup (¼ liter) cold water. When thoroughly mixed, add 4 tablespoons *ammonia and 4 tablespoons *turpentine, then shake the mixture well. Bottle and keep well corked. Shake before use.

Or make a paste of tailor's chalk and *denatured alcohol, or water mixed with a few drops of *ammonia. Apply the paste to the silver as usual and rub clean with a soft cloth.

Silver Polishing Cloths

Mix 1 cup (¼ liter) water with silver paste and soak old towels in the mixture. When saturated, hang the cloths up to dry without squeezing. Use these cloths to dry silver after washing.

Stainless Steel

Rub stains with a paste made of tailor's chalk and water, then wash in hot soapy water; rinse well and dry.

Do not use chemical cleaners or silver polish.

Zinc

To clean zinc, rub with a mixture of salt and white vinegar, or half a lemon dipped in salt. Rinse well and dry thoroughly and polish with a soft cloth.

Leather
Leather
Leather
Leather
Leather
Leather
Leather
Leather
Leather

Bookbindings

See Leather Bookbindings in Paper section (page 40).

Household Chamois Cloths

Soak the dirty cloths in 1 qt. (1 liter) warm water and add a small piece of washing soda and leave for an hour. Wash and rinse in warm water, then gently wring out the excess water and hang up to dry, occasionally pulling and rubbing it into shape.

Ingrained Dirt

Rub the article with a damp cloth and saddle soap and work up a lather, then wipe off the soap and allow the leather to dry slowly and thoroughly. Then polish with furniture cream (see page 21). Saddle soap is not a polish, only a cleaner.

Always use a cream polish after using the soap to make the leather supple. The leather will crack if the soap is used on its own.

Leather Dressing

Mix two parts boiled linseed oil with one part white vinegar in a bottle. Keep tightly corked and shake well before use. Use only a little on a soft cloth and rub well into the leather, then polish with a soft clean cloth. Excellent for constant use on upholstery and other leather articles in good condition.

Leather Upholstery

Polish leather upholstery with leather dressing.

Polish smooth and rough grain leathers with furniture polish.

Leather Wear and Tear

To prevent wear and tear and to make old leather supple, rub with any of the following: petroleum jelly, lanolin, castor oil or olive oil. (Do not use *kerosene or linseed oil.) The oils sink into the leather more easily if warmed. Repeat this application frequently, then polish with a soft cloth. If the leather is very old and hard, apply the oil and then rub with a rag dipped in *turpentine.

Morocco Leather
Varnish with egg white to restore the luster.

Patent Leather
Remove any dust or mud when dry with a very soft brush, then rub the whole surface with petroleum jelly and polish with a clean cloth.

To remove finger marks, rub the surface with cold milk, then dry and polish with a soft cloth.

Polishing Hint
It is important not to use too much polish, to prevent permanent staining. When using liquid dressing, immerse a clean rag in the dressing and wring out the excess liquid before use.

Powdery Leather
Paint powdery leather with a mixture of castor oil and *denatured alcohol in a 60–40 volume mixture, and leave for twenty-four hours. Then apply pure castor oil to make the leather supple.

Suede
Dip a clean cloth in ground oatmeal and rub in a circular motion into greasy stains, then brush out all the powder gently with a wire brush. Repeat the process if necessary. This will not harm the suede.

Or brush greasy stains with lemon juice and a wire brush, then hold in the steam of a boiling kettle for a few minutes and brush dry with a wire brush.

In all cases, test an unimportant area first and if in any doubt seek expert advice.

Smear very shabby suede with plenty of boot polish and brush into the whole surface very hard. Repeat this several times over a period of days. This will moisten the skin and give the article the appearance of soft kid leather. Polish to a sheen with a soft cloth.

SHOES AND BOOTS

Black and Brown Shoes
Rub black shoes with the inside of the rind of a fresh orange, then polish as usual. Rub brown shoes with the inside of a banana skin, then polish as usual.

Drying Shoes
Always dry leather slowly and thoroughly, away from direct heat. Stuff the article with crumpled newspaper to keep its shape and leave to dry in an airy place. The leather must always be completely dry before polishing or oiling.

Shoe Polish
Shred 2 tablespoons (30 grams) white candle wax into an old pan and place it into another pan filled with water. Bring it to the boil until the wax melts. Add 4 tablespoons *turpentine and mix together thoroughly.

Shred 1 tablespoon (15 grams) castile soap or pure soap flakes and mix into a thick paste with ½ cup (115 grams) boiling water. Cool the mixtures and mix them together while still liquid, and beat hard. Add soot to the mixture for black shoes. Store the polish in jars.

Waterproofing
Stand the leather soles in boiled linseed oil until they are

saturated, then drain and leave to dry. Rub the uppers with castor oil.

A cheap and easy method is to varnish the soles and allow the varnish to dry slowly.

LEATHER STAINS

Creaking Shoes
Soak the soles in salt water, then dry slowly and thoroughly. Leave for twelve hours in boiled linseed oil, then drain and dry. This will stop the soles from creaking.

Grease
To remove grease stains from leather, rub the stain with a thick paste made of fuller's earth and water. Leave to dry and brush off the powder. Repeat the process if necessary, then polish as usual. This is harmless to the leather and will not remove the color.

Ink
To remove ink stains, cover the stain with damp bicarbonate of soda and change the powder as it discolors until the stain has gone. Then dry well and polish as usual.

Mildew
Rub mildew stains with petroleum jelly, then polish as usual.

Rainwater
Rub rainwater marks with a little *denatured alcohol, then polish as usual.

Salt Water
Rub salt water stains with a mixture of 1 cup hot milk mixed with a small piece of washing soda, dry slowly and repeat if necessary. If the stain has turned black, mix equal

parts of *ammonia and milk and rub the stain gently, then dry slowly and thoroughly. If the leather is hard after drying, rub with castor oil, then polish as usual.

Paper
Paper
Paper
Paper
Paper
Paper

Books

To remove greasy finger marks from cloth book covers, rub with stale bread or a soft India eraser.

To remove greasy marks from printed music sheets and paper, make a thick paste of fuller's earth and a little water. Spread the mixture thickly over the stain with a knife blade and leave for several hours to dry thoroughly, then brush the powder off.

To remove ink stains, gently dampen with warm water using a soft-haired paintbrush. Blot up excess inky water. Then wet the stain again with a 5% solution of *oxalic acid. Paint with warm water and dry with white blotting paper, then air well and press gently. If in doubt seek expert advice.

Envelopes

Envelopes sealed with egg whites cannot be steamed open.

Leather Book Bindings

To restore leather bound books, use Goddard's Saddler's Wax with cheese cloth.

Parchment and Vellum

Sponge the surface very gently with *lighter fluid to remove grease marks and spots. This will not harm the material, but if in doubt test on an unimportant area or seek expert advice.

Photographs

To clean old photographs, rub gently with stale bread.

Playing Cards

Rub the surface with a soft cloth dipped in a weak solution of camphor oil and warm water.

Prints and Mounting Cards

Always ask a framer to mount prints, drawings and watercolors on heavy cardboard which is made of rags and prevents the buildup of acids. These cause discoloration and deterioration. Wood-pulp boards allow the buildup of acids.

Wallpaper

To remove grease spots on wallpaper, place a piece of clean blotting paper over the mark and press with a warm iron. Repeat until the spot has gone.

To strip wallpaper, wet the paper with warm water mixed with a little liquid detergent and let the solution soak in, then gently peel the paper off the wall. This works as well as a store-bought stripper.

Ornaments
Ornaments
Ornaments
Ornaments
Ornaments
Ornaments
Ornaments
Ornaments
Ornaments
Ornaments
Ornaments

Alabaster

*Gasoline, *kerosene, *lighter fluid and *nail polish remover are all safe to use as stain removers. Apply with a soft cloth and rub the stain gently.

Never use water on alabaster.

Amber

Wash the article in warm milk or soap and water. Dry and polish with a soft cloth.

Coral

Wash the article in a basin of warm soapy water and polish with tissue paper. If very dirty, boil the article carefully in soapy water with a little washing soda.

Ebony

Wipe the article with a damp cloth, then cover with linseed oil and polish with a soft cloth.

Ivory and Piano Keys

To clean and polish ivory, rub gently in the direction of the grain with a fine abrasive paste. Either *lighter fluid or *gasoline mixed with finely powdered tailor's chalk, or lemon juice and whiting are suitable. Apply the paste with a damp chamois cloth and leave to dry. Then gently brush the powder off and polish with a soft cloth.

Never use water on ivory and where possible leave exposed to sunlight as ivory yellows in the dark.

Japan

Wipe the article with warm water and soap, then dry and dredge in dry flour, leave for one hour, then dust and polish with a soft cloth.

Jet

To clean carved jet, rub the article with finely ground

bread crumbs. Then polish with a soft cloth.

To clean jet beads, rub with warm olive oil, then polish with a soft cloth.

Lacquer
To restore the gloss to dull lacquered articles, dip them in warm water with lemon juice or sour milk, then rub with a soft cloth. Dry in a warm place and polish with a chamois cloth.

If very dirty, apply a paste made of flour and olive oil. Rub in well with a cloth, then wipe off and polish with a silk rag.

Marble
To clean marble, wash with good quality soap and water, using a brush. For less important pieces add a little *ammonia to the water. Dry well and polish.

To polish marble, rub the surface with powdered chalk moistened with water. Or sift two parts washing soda, one part powdered pumice stone and one part powdered chalk and mix into a paste with water. Rub into the marble and leave for twenty-four hours. Then wash off with soapy water, dry and polish with a soft cloth.

Unlike alabaster, marble will not be harmed by water, but acids dissolve marble and should be used with great care.

Rust stains can be removed with a 5% solution of *oxalic acid or lemon juice. Then polish as usual. Oil stains can be removed by applying a paste made of powdered kaolin and *gasoline. Cover the stain and leave to dry, then wipe off and polish with a soft cloth.

Ormolu
To clean ormolu, scrub with soapy water and a little *ammonia. Rinse well in clean water and dry thoroughly.

To remove lacquer from ormolu, rub with a solvent like
*denatured alcohol.

Papier-Mâché

Sponge all papier-mâché articles with cold water without
soap, then dredge in flour while still damp. When dry,
polish with a soft cloth.

Never use hot water as it will crack the varnish.

Pearls

Never wash artificial pearls. Just rub them with tissue
paper to give them an extra sheen.

Wash real pearls in very salty water. Then polish them
with a velvet cloth. If in doubt seek expert advice.

Plaster Statuettes

To remove dirt and grease, mix a paste of finely powdered
starch and hot water. Apply the paste when hot with a
brush to the plaster. Leave to dry. When dry, the starch
will split and flake off. The grease and dirt will be
absorbed by the starch.

Tortoiseshell and Horn

Rub articles by hand with petroleum jelly, olive oil or
linseed oil. Then polish off excess oil with a soft cloth.
Horn can be rubbed with a damp cloth before oiling.

Glass
Glass
Glass
Glass
Glass

Annealing Glass

Immerse the glass in a pan of cold water, then slowly heat until it is boiling. Remove the pan from the heat and leave to cool. This will protect the glass from cracking in very hot water, but if the glass is to be exposed to higher temperatures, boil in oil instead of water.

Bottles

To clean oily bottles, fill them with fine ashes and place in a pan of cold water. Gradually heat the water till it boils, then simmer for thirty minutes. When cool, wash out the ashes with cold running water, wash in hot soapy water, then rinse and dry.

Crystal

Cover the shelves used for storing crystal with felt or thick paper, to prevent the glass from chipping or cracking.

Decanters

To clean decanters, fill with warm water and add 1 tablespoon baking powder and some crushed eggshells. Leave for twelve hours, stirring occasionally. Then rinse with warm water and a little *ammonia.

To remove wine stains from decanters, pour about two inches white vinegar into the decanter and add 1 teaspoon scouring powder, then fill the decanter with fairly hot water. Shake it vigorously and leave to soak overnight, then shake again, rinse well and wash in hot soapy water. Rinse again and dry.

Glassware

When washing valuable pieces of glass, place a thick towel in the bottom of the washing bowl.

When cut glass clouds and ordinary washing does not clean it, cover the glass with wet potato peelings and leave for twenty-four hours. Then rinse in cold water and dry.

Mirrors, Windows and Picture Glass

To clean the glass, rub gently with a soft rag dipped in
*turpentine, *denatured alcohol or *kerosene. Then
polish with crumpled newspaper to give a brilliant sheen.

To prevent glass from steaming up, wipe with a soft cloth
and a little glycerine after cleaning and drying.

To make windows opaque temporarily, dissolve 2
tablespoons Epsom salts in 2 cups (½ liter) water and
apply the mixture evenly with a sponge.

To remove fly stains from glass, wipe with a woolen cloth
dipped in *denatured alcohol.

To remove dried paint from windows, rub the paint with
the edge of a coin. When all the paint has been scraped
away, wipe the window with a damp cloth and polish with
a chamois cloth. To remove paint spots from glass, rub
vigorously with any of the following: linseed oil, hot white
vinegar, *turpentine or a strong solution of washing soda.

Thermos Bottles

Fill the thermos three-quarters full with warm water and
add 1 teaspoon bicarbonate of soda. Replace the stopper
and shake vigorously, then rinse well and dry. This will
remove the musty smell.

Kitchen Things
Kitchen Things
Kitchen Things
Kitchen Things
Kitchen Things
Kitchen Things
Kitchen Things
Kitchen Things
Kitchen Things
Kitchen Things
Kitchen Things
Kitchen Things
Kitchen Things
Kitchen Things

Aluminum Saucepans

Fill burned aluminum pans with cold water, add 2 tablespoons bicarbonate of soda and slowly bring to the boil. Simmer for fifteen minutes. The burned food will rub off easily. If the stains are very stubborn, repeat the process and simmer for a longer time.

Never use washing soda.

If stained, cook rhubarb or apple peelings in the pan.

Cake and Steel Pans

Cover new cake pans, baking trays and steel pans with a layer of lard and place in a hot oven until the grease melts and soaks into the surface. Remove from the oven and cool, then wash in warm soapy water and dry thoroughly. This will season the metal and prevent rusting and sticking.

Carbon Steel Knives

Wipe the blade clean with a hot damp cloth, and dry immediately. Rub with grease if the knife is not in constant use.

Sharpen with a steel, a stone or an electric knife sharpener.

Remove stains and rust marks by rubbing the blade with a damp piece of very fine emery paper, followed by onion juice. Rinse well and dry thoroughly.

Enamel Pans

To clean white enamel pans, rub the surface with bicarbonate of soda and wash in hot soapsuds. Rinse well and dry thoroughly.

To prevent enameled pans from burning and discoloring, place an asbestos mat over the gas or electric ring during heating.

Garbage Cans

Burn straw or newpaper in galvanized garbage cans to remove any grease or dampness.

Gummed Labels

Rub the labels with *acetone to remove the gum.

Electric Kettles

To "de-fur," dissolve 2 teaspoons borax in the kettle full of water and boil for fifteen minutes, then rinse well.

Cut off a small piece of loofah and place inside the kettle to collect up the deposits during use. When encrusted, remove the loofah and rinse it well. Save the sediment to clean any enamel goods and replace the loofah inside the kettle.

A marble kept inside the kettle will prevent the furring deposits from sticking to the sides.

Knife Handles

Never immerse knife handles in the dishwater as it loosens the blades and discolors the wood or bone.

Pan Lids

If the knob comes off a pan lid, insert a screw through the hole from the back of the lid and twist on a wine cork.

Refrigerators

Never clean refrigerators with disinfectant as it will make the food taste of it, and leave a strong smell. Wash the inside with warm water and some bicarbonate of soda, then rinse well with clean water and dry.

Saltshakers

Smear the salt spots on plated saltshakers with olive oil and leave for several days, then clean as usual.

Scouring Pads

Cut a loofah lengthwise, then cut each half into six. These are much gentler to the hands than steel wool and will not rust.

Collect nylon net fruit bags and put several pieces inside one of the bags and close the end with a piece of string.

Storage Containers

Fill storage jars or plastic containers with tepid water, add a few drops of vanilla extract and leave to soak for forty-eight hours. Rinse well and dry thoroughly. This will remove any musty smells.

Teapots

Rub the inside of musty smelling teapots and coffee pots with salt and vinegar, then rinse thoroughly with plenty of warm water.

Laundry Hints
Laundry Hints
Laundry Hints
Laundry Hints
Laundry Hints
Laundry Hints
Laundry Hints
Laundry Hints
Laundry Hints
Laundry Hints
Laundry Hints
Laundry Hints
Laundry Hints
Laundry Hints
Laundry Hints
Laundry Hints

Bleaching

Do not use on wool, silk, leather, resin-coated cotton, linen or rayon fabrics that are already weak.

Always test on an unimportant area of fabric before using.

To bleach untreated white cotton, linen and some synthetics, add 1 cup bleach to 1 gallon (4 liters) cold water and mix thoroughly. Soak the article for no longer than thirty minutes, then rinse very thoroughly.

To make a mild solution to remove stains from washable materials, add 2 tablespoons (30 grams) bleach to 1 qt. (1 liter) cold water and apply it with a medicine dropper, or soak the article in the solution for fifteen minutes. In both cases rinse out the bleach thoroughly. Repeat the process if necessary.

Mix 1 teaspoon bleach in a cup of cold water to remove stains from nonwashable fabrics. Apply with a dropper and leave for fifteen minutes, then sponge thoroughly with plenty of water.

To make a strong solution for stubborn stains, mix equal parts of bleach and water and apply with a dropper. Rinse immediately with plenty of water and repeat if necessary.

To remove stains in washable fabrics, dissolve 2 tablespoons (30 grams) sodium perborate in 2 cups (½ liter) hot water and soak the article for twelve hours. Then rinse out thoroughly. Use lukewarm water for silks and wool.

Apply the above solution with a medicine dropper to the stain on nonwashable fabrics and keep the stain damp for several hours until it disappears, then sponge thoroughly with plenty of water.

Bleaching Liquid

Dissolve 1 tablespoon borax in 1 qt. (1 liter) boiling water, then add 1 qt. (1 liter) cold water. Dip the stained fabric into the solution and dry in the sun. Repeat the process until the stain has disappeared, then rinse the article well in clean water. Test first.

Branwater

Tie 1½ cups bran in a piece of cotton cloth and place in a pan with 1 qt. (1 liter) water, and bring to the boil. Simmer for half an hour and strain. Add 2 cups (½ liter) lukewarm water to the solution and stir well. This is good for washing fine blouses and gaily colored fabrics, and no soap is needed.

Dilute the mixture to rinse articles in. Do not starch the fabrics as the bran acts as a stiffener when the material is ironed.

Carbolic Soap

Add ½ tablespoon carbolic to 2½ lbs. (1¼ kilograms) of the mixture and stir well and pour into molds as above. This is a good disinfectant soap.

Fireproofing

Dissolve ¼ cup (60 grams) alum in 1 gallon (4 liters) water and dip the fabric in the solution and dry.

Gum Arabic Starch

Dissolve ¼ cup (60 grams) white gum arabic powder in 2 cups (½ liter) boiling water, cover and leave for twelve hours. Then pour the solution into clean bottles, leaving the dregs behind. Add 1 tablespoon of the mixture to 2 cups (½ liter) starch when ironing cotton, lawn and lace.

Dilute the solution with water for stiffening white muslin.

Honey Soap

Shred 2 lbs. (900 kilograms) yellow soap into a double saucepan and melt. Add ½ cup (115 grams) palm oil, ½ cup (115 grams) honey and a few drops of cinnamon oil.

Bring to the boil and simmer for six to eight minutes, then pour into molds and allow to set. It will be ready for use the following day and is a very superior soap for washing clothes and yourself.

Invisible Mending
To make an invisible mend, sew with a long human hair instead of cotton. Particularly effective on tweed.

Keeping Colors Fast
Add 1 teaspoon Epsom salts to each gallon (4 liters) water used for washing and rinsing.

Plain Household Soap
Pour 2½ lbs. (1¼ kilograms) of the mixture into a straight-sided wooden box lined with a wet cloth, and leave to set. Then cut into squares and allow to dry thoroughly before use. It can be colored and scented if desired.

Sand Soap
Add 3 lbs. (1½ kilograms) fine sand to 4 lbs. (1¾ kilograms) of the mixture and pour into molds as above. This is an abrasive scouring soap suitable for floors and stone steps.

Scorch Mixture
Peel, slice and pound one large onion and mix it with 1 cup (¼ liter) white vinegar, ¼ cup (60 grams) washing soda and ¼ cup (60 grams) fuller's earth, and boil for ten minutes. Then strain the mixture and store in well-corked bottles. Spread a little of the mixture on the scorch mark and leave to dry. Repeat the process until the mark has gone.

Setting New Colors
Soak the new articles for several hours in the following:

Blue fabrics: Add 1½ cups white vinegar to 1 gallon (4 liters) water.

Brown, gray and pink fabrics: Add 1½ cups salt and 1 teaspoon alum to 1 gallon (4 liters) water.

Green fabrics: Add ½ cup (115 grams) alum to 3 gallons (12 liters) water.

Checked and patterned fabrics: Add ½ cup white vinegar, 1 cup salt and 1 tablespoon alum to 1 gallon (4 liters) water.

After soaking, hang the fabric in the shade to dry, without wringing, then wash in the usual way.

Soap Jelly or Soft Soap

Used for washing silks, satins, lace and colored woolens.

Collect all old ends of soaps and shred into pan. Cover with boiling water and leave to dissolve, then stir well.

The mixture should be allowed to cool until it is thick enough to be lifted in the hands, so more soap or water may need to be added to obtain the right consistency. Make the soap the day before use, to allow it to set.

Soaps

Soap and water is the only cleaning agent that is equally effective in dealing with sugary, sticky and greasy substances.

Softening Hard Water

For the best washing results use soft water.

Hard water is softened by adding an alkali: 2 to 3 tablespoons per gallon (4 liters) is an approximate guide depending on the hardness of the water. Washing soda, *ammonia and borax are all effective.

Or add ½ cup (115 grams) rose water, ¼ cup (60 grams)

pure brandy and ¼ cup (60 grams) lemon juice to 2 qts. (2 liters) water. Mix together and store in well-corked bottles. When washing, add 2 tablespoons of the mixture to 1 gallon (4 liters) of water to soften it.

Starching

Starching helps to prevent fabrics from getting badly soiled. All natural starches are insoluble in cold water and can only be dissolved by soaking in boiling water.

Stitchless Mending

Place the damaged area of the fabric on a flat surface, wrong side up. Spread the area with egg white and cover the tear with a piece of fine linen slightly larger than the rip, and press with a hot iron to make the egg stick. This will be almost invisible if done before fraying starts.

Fabrics
Fabrics
Fabrics
Fabrics
Fabrics
Fabrics
Fabrics
Fabrics

Black Cloth

To remove the sheen from black cloth, rub the area with a sponge dipped in *turpentine and air well outside.

Chiffon

Wash the article in lukewarm soapy water. Squeeze gently until clean (do not rub), then rinse well. Lay the garment flat on a large towel and pull gently into shape. Place another towel on top and roll up. When almost dry, press with a warm iron.

Chintz

Wash the article in lukewarm soapy water and rinse well. Then add 2 teaspoons powdered size to 1 cup (¼ liter) boiling water. Make sure the size is completely dissolved, then strain. Dip the garment into the solution and squeeze out the excess. Roll in a towel to dry partially, then press lightly with a warm iron.

Stiff hot starch can be used if size is not available. Follow the instructions on the packet.

Branwater (see page 57) can be used instead of soap to prevent chintz fading.

Never use washing soda to wash chintz.

Comforters

Wash down-filled comforters individually in a washing machine with hot water and soap. Rinse well and tumble-dry. When thoroughly dry, shake vigorously to fluff up the feathers.

Never dry-clean down-filled comforters.

Follow the manufacturer's advice for comforters filled with man-made fiber.

Cotton

Wash white cotton in very hot soapy water. A mild

*chlorine bleach can be added to the wash if necessary. Rinse well in clean water and wring or spin dry. Press with a hot iron while still damp. Starch if necessary.

Colored cottons can be washed together providing the colors are fast. Add salt to the water to prevent the colors from running and wash as above.

Never use strong detergents to wash cottons.

Wash drip-dry cottons in plenty of hot water. Do not squeeze as this causes creases. When clean, hang up and pull the garment into shape and leave to drip-dry.

Damask

To clean damask covers, rub warm bran well into the fabric with a clean cloth and keep changing the cloth. When clean, brush out all the bran with a soft brush.

Furs

To clean dark furs, heat a quantity of bran in a pan, and stir it continuously to prevent it from burning. Rub the warm bran well into the fur by hand, then shake it out.

Repeat the process until the bran appears clean, then shake and brush the fur to remove all the bran. This method can also be used for Angora rugs.

To gloss the edges, rub with a cloth dipped in *denatured alcohol.

To clean light colored furs, first rub in damp warm bran with a dry cloth, until the bran is dry. Then shake the fur well and rub in dry warmed bran with a piece of white muslin, and shake again. Then rub in powdered magnesia against the way of the fur until clean. Shake and brush well to remove all the powders. If in doubt, consult an expert.

Georgette

Wash in warm pure white soap flakes, and squeeze gently by hand. Lift the article up and down in the water, taking care not to strain the fabric. When clean, rinse in warm water and repeat until the water is clear. Gently squeeze out the excess water and roll in a thick towel. Press, when damp, with a warm iron.

Lace

Handle lace with care. Always squeeze the fabric when washing, never rub it.

Wash white lace in pure soap flakes and hot water mixed together to make a thick lather. Pour the soap solution into a jar and add the lace, then cover the jar and shake it for five minutes. Change the soap and repeat the process until the lace is clean. Rinse well in warm, then cold water.

Then dissolve 1 teaspoon gum arabic starch (see page 57) in 2 cups (½ liter) water and dip the lace into it. Squeeze out the excess water and roll in a thick towel. Lay the lace flat, face down on a damp ironing board and pull it into shape, then pin it. Cover with a damp cloth and press with a cool iron.

To freshen black lace, dissolve a few drops of *ammonia in 2 cups (½ liter) water and gently sponge the lace with the solution until it is damp. Roll the lace in a cloth and leave for half an hour, then press as above.

Never wash black lace.

Store valuable lace in blue tissue paper to preserve its color.

Lambskins

To clean lambskins, rub in plenty of powdered magnesia by hand and leave overnight. Then shake and brush until all the powder is removed.

If in any doubt when cleaning furs consult an expert.

Linen

White linen sheets, napkins and tablecloths can be washed like white cotton.

Natural colored linen needs gentler treatment. Wash in cooler water and do not bleach.

Wash dyed linen carefully, squeezing the fabric as little as possible.

Press all linens while damp with a fairly hot iron.

Man-Made Fibers

Follow the manufacturer's instructions for washing.

Muslin

Add 1 teaspoon salt to a bucket of cold water and soak the garment in it for half an hour. Then add 1 tablespoon soap jelly (see page 59) to a basin of warm water, and beat into a lather. Wash the article in the solution by kneading and squeezing, then repeat the process in a fresh soap solution until clean. Mix a little white vinegar or starch to warm water and rinse the garment well in it.

Starch slightly and iron when damp with a warm iron.

Satin

Add ½ tablespoon *kerosene to every quart of warm soapy water needed to immerse the article. Lift the garment up and down in the mixture until clean. Then rinse several times in clear warm water and add a little borax to the final rinse to restore the gloss. Squeeze out the excess water and partially dry, then press on the wrong side with a warm iron.

Serge

Wash a handful of ivy leaves and place in an old pan,

adding 1 qt. (1 liter) water. Bring to the boil and simmer
for twenty minutes, then strain and store in well-corked
bottles. Sponge the shiny areas of black and navy serge
with the mixture to eliminate the sheen.

Silk

Completely dissolve pure soap flakes in hand hot water
and add the garment. Agitate gently and repeat the
process with clean suds. Rinse well in warm, then cold,
water. Add 1 or 2 tablespoons gum arabic starch to every
gallon (4 liters) water used in the final rinse, to stiffen the
silk. Then squeeze out the excess water and roll in a thick
towel. Press while damp with a warm iron. Rewet the silk
rather than sprinkle with water if it is too dry to iron, as
sprinkled water can mark the fabric.

Do not stiffen shantung silk.

Velvet

Add a little *ammonia to a pan of boiling water and hold
the velvet pile down over the steam. Then hold the damp
fabric over a hot iron to raise the pile and freshen.

Gently rub grease marks with a cloth dipped in
*turpentine until dry. Repeat if necessary. Then brush
lightly and hang outside to air.

Viyella

Wash Viyella as for wool (see below).

Iron with a fairly hot iron when almost dry, on the right
side for light colors and the wrong side for dark colors.

Wool

General rules:

Wash woolens in hand-hot water. Avoid extremes of
temperature or they will shrink.

Do not soak woolens or leave wet.

Do not rub, twist or wring the fabric.

Do not use *ammonia or too much soap and always rinse well.

Do not machine-wash unless specifically stated on the manufacturer's washing instructions.

Wash wool in hand-hot water with pure soap flakes. Dissolve the soap completely before adding the garment. Agitate gently and repeat the process in clean suds. Rinse thoroughly in warm water, and add salt if the colors are likely to run.

Squeeze out excess water or spin-dry for a few minutes. Arrange garment on a hanger and pull gently into shape, or lay flat on a thick towel to dry. Cover the dry article with a damp cloth and press with a warm iron if necessary, and air well.

Wool (Angora)
To prevent Angora wool from shedding, place the garment in a plastic bag and leave in the refrigerator overnight. The effect will last for twenty-four hours.

FABRIC STAINS

General Rules
Remove stains as soon as possible.

Consider the composition of fabric as well as the type of stain.

Try the least harmful method first. Always test chemical solvents on an unimportant area of the fabric first.

After using chemicals, rinse the fabric well.

After using bleach, boil the article if possible and dry outside.

After using acids, neutralize the effect with an alkali rinse.

Strong acids and alkalis should only be used in weak solutions mixed with warm water (never boiling water) as they are harmful to certain materials, e.g., wool and woolen mixtures, silks, nylons, Orlon and all colored materials.

See Glossary, pages 84–86 for acids and alkalis.

Do not use nail polish remover on acetates, rayon or polyester.

Do not use grease solvents, except soap, on plastics.

Do not use *oxalic acid on silks or wool.

Acid

To restore the color to fabrics faded by acid, sponge with a little *ammonia and water.

Alcohol

Washable fabrics: Rinse in clear warm water until the stain has gone, then wash as usual. White linen and cotton can be bleached if necessary.

Nonwashable fabrics: Rinse with clear warm water, and dry well.

Beer

Washable fabrics: Ordinary washing often removes the stain, but if ineffective, rewash the garment adding a little white vinegar or *ammonia to warm soapy water. Then rinse well and dry.

Nonwashable fabrics: Sponge the stain with *denatured alcohol, then rub a little hard soap into the mark and leave to dry. When dry, brush the fabric well.

Blood

Washable fabrics: Soak freshly stained fabrics in cold

water, then wash with soap and cold water and rinse well. Bleach white fabrics if necessary and soak silks in a borax-and-water solution of ¼ cup to 2 cups (60 grams to ½ liter) and rinse well. Then wash all fabrics as usual.

Soak old dried bloodstained fabrics in biodegradable laundry detergent and cold water overnight, or add 2 cups (½ liter) salt to 1 gallon (4 liters) cold water and soak article for up to twelve hours. Bleach white fabrics after soaking if necessary. Then wash all fabrics as usual.

Nonwashable fabrics: Sponge the stain with cold water. Then make a paste of starch and cold water and spread it on thickly, leaving it to dry and absorb the stain. When dry, brush off lightly with a soft brush. This is harmless even to delicate fabrics.

Cocoa and Chocolate

Washable fabrics: Sponge the stain with cold water. Never use hot water. Then add 2 tablespoons (30 grams) borax to 2 cups (½ liter) warm water, and sponge the stain with the solution. Then rinse well and wash the article as usual.

Nonwashable fabrics: Sponge the mark with *carbon tetrachloride, testing the fabric first in an unimportant area. Then sponge again with the above borax solution.

Coffee

Washable fabrics: Sponge fresh stains with the above borax solution. Then rinse, and wash as usual.

Sponge old stains with cold water, then rub well with glycerine. Leave for half an hour and rinse with warm water. Bleach white fabrics if necessary. Then wash all fabrics as usual.

Nonwashable fabrics: Sponge the fabric with clear warm water or the above borax solution and rub dry. If any stain is left, sponge with a grease solvent (see Glossary, pages 87–89).

Egg

Washable fabrics: Soak the fabric in a warm solution of biodegradable laundry detergent and water. Then wash as usual.

Nonwashable fabrics: Sponge the stain with the above solution.

Fruit and Fruit Juice

Washable fabrics: If the stain is fresh, stretch the fabric over a basin and pour boiling water through the stain from a height. Then wash as usual.

Or cover the stain with dry starch and leave for one hour, then brush off and wash the garment as usual.

Rub old stains with glycerine and leave for one hour. Pour boiling water through the stain and repeat the process if necessary. Then wash as usual.

Nonwashable fabrics: Sponge the stain with cold water, then glycerine, and leave for one hour, and rub with a grease solvent (see Glossary, pages 87–89).

Grass

Washable fabrics: Wash in hot suds when possible, or sponge the stain with *denatured alcohol, then wash as usual.

Sponge nylons and synthetics with a solution of equal parts warm water and *denatured alcohol and rinse well, then wash as usual.

Rub severe stains with glycerine and leave for one hour, then wash as usual.

Nonwashable fabrics: Sponge the stain with *denatured alcohol or eucalyptus oil, then wipe with a cloth dipped in clean water, and pat dry.

Gravy

Wash or sponge with lukewarm detergent suds.

Soak old or severe stains in cool salt water mixed with a little *ammonia, then wash in cool suds.

Never wash gravy stains with hot water.

Grease and Oil

Washable fabrics: Wash the article in very hot liquid detergent if possible. If not, place a clean cloth or blotting paper under the stain and sponge with *carbon tetrachloride or *gasoline. Then wash and rinse thoroughly.

Nonwashable fabrics: Sponge the fabric on the wrong side with *gasoline or *carbon tetrachloride. Test the fabric first to make sure it is not badly affected by the solvents.

Ink

Washable fabrics: Soak fresh stains immediately in cold water.

Sponge white fabrics, after soaking, with a 5% solution of *oxalic acid and warm water. Then rinse well and wash as usual.

Dip old stains on white fabrics in cold water, then cover the stain with a paste of cream of tartar and lemon juice and leave for one hour. Rinse thoroughly and wash as usual.

Sponge colored fabrics with *gasoline or *turpentine, then rinse well and wash in liquid detergent.

Nonwashable fabrics: Apply the same solutions and recipes as above with a sponge, then pat dry with a cloth.

Inks (Ballpoint and Felt-Tip Pen)

Drip *denatured alcohol or *carbon tetrachloride onto

the stain. First test the solvents on an unimportant area to make sure they do not harm the fabric. When the ink has dissolved, rub with a clean cloth dipped in more of the alcohol. Repeat the process with a clean cloth until the stain has gone.

Lipstick

Washable fabrics: Scrape off as much as possible with a blunt knife, then wash in hot liquid detergent.

Rub severe stains with glycerine, eucalyptus oil or petroleum jelly before washing.

Nonwashable fabrics: Sponge with a grease solvent (see Glossary, pages 87–89).

Mildew

Wash newly formed stains in hot soapy water as soon as possible, then rinse and dry outside.

For obstinate stains on white fabrics, soak in a solution of one part chlorine bleach to eight parts cold water for about ten minutes. Then wring out the water and place the article in a weak solution of cold water and white vinegar to neutralize the bleaching action. Rinse well and wash as usual.

Milk

Washable fabrics: Rinse the fabric in cool water, then wash with cold liquid detergent suds.

Soak stains in delicate fabrics in equal parts of glycerine and warm water and rub gently. When the stain is loose, wash in tepid soapy water, then rinse and dry. Or soak the stain in *denatured alcohol for about two minutes, then wash with soap jelly (see page 59).

Nonwashable fabrics: Sponge the stain with *denatured alcohol, then dab with cold water.

Mud

Washable fabrics: Allow the mud to dry, then brush off the excess with a soft brush. Rub the remaining stain with boiled potato water or a weak solution of borax: 2 tablespoons (30 grams) borax to 2 cups (½ liter) water, then rinse well and wash as usual.

Nonwashable fabrics: Allow mud to dry and brush off as much as possible. Rub the remaining stain with *carbon tetrachloride. Test the fabric first to make sure it is not harmed by the solvent.

Nail Polish

Before attempting to remove the stain with any of the following chemicals, test the fabric first in an unimportant area to avoid damage.

Protect work surfaces as *acetone will damage paint and varnish.

Washable fabrics: Sponge fresh stains with *acetone or *nail polish remover and wipe with a clean cloth until the stain fades.

Dampen old stains on rayon with a little *carbon tetrachloride, then drip *amyl acetate on to the softened stain, and wipe with a clean cloth. *Acetone can be used after the *carbon tetrachloride, except on rayon. Finally, wash with warm soapy water.

Nonwashable fabrics: Follow the above process, but do not wash. Instead, dab the affected area with *denatured alcohol and wipe dry with a soft cloth.

Paints

Enamel paint: Sponge the stains with *turpentine or mix equal parts of *ammonia and *turpentine. Soak the garment until the stain has dissolved, then wash in the usual way in soapy suds.

Soften dried enamel paint stains with two parts of
*ammonia mixed with one part *turpentine or *kerosene
and rub into the marks, then wipe clean with a cloth and
dry.

Emulsion paint: Soak or sponge fresh stains with cold
water, then wash in the usual way.

Perfume
Washable fabrics: Wash fresh stains immediately in warm
clear water. Rub dry stains with glycerine, then wash as
usual.

Nonwashable fabrics: Rub the stain with glycerine and
leave for one hour, then rinse by sponging with clean
warm water.

Perspiration
Sponge the stains with any of the following: A weak
solution of white vinegar and water, or lemon juice; or
dissolve two aspirins in water and soak the article; or soak
the article in a mild solution of liquid detergent. In all
cases, rinse very well, then wash as usual.

Rust
Stretch stained white linen and cotton over a bowl and
pour boiling water from a height through the stain. Then
cover the mark with a paste of cream of tartar and lemon
juice and rinse quickly in water containing a little
*ammonia. Repeat if necessary, then wash and boil the
garment.

Soak colored fabrics in a little lemon juice or sour milk
and leave for two or three minutes. Then rinse thoroughly
and wash as usual.

Seawater
Rub the fabric with white vinegar to restore the color.

Brush dried stains to remove the salt, then soak in warm

water until all the salt has dissolved. Rinse and wash as usual. Repeat the process if necessary.

Toffee (Candy)
Soak the stained fabric in warm water to dissolve the sugar. Add a few drops of *denatured alcohol and a little white vinegar to the water if the stain is very obstinate. Rinse well, then wash as usual.

Tar
Scrape off the thick surface tar with a blunt knife, then soften the remaining stain with butter or lard, and rub with *turpentine or *gasoline or *kerosene. Do not use water as this makes it spread.

Sponge delicate fabrics with oil of eucalyptus. Then in all cases wash as usual.

Tea
Washable fabrics: Pour boiling water over stains in white fabrics while still fresh. Bleach if necessary, and add a little vinegar to the final rinse, then wash as usual.

Colored fabrics: Sponge colored fabrics with a warm borax solution: 2 tablespoons (30 grams) borax to 2 cups (½ liter) water, and rub the stain hard. Rinse thoroughly and wash as usual.

Nonwashable fabrics: Rub the stain with glycerine and leave for one hour, then sponge with *carbon tetrachloride or *denatured alcohol. Test the fabric first in an unimportant area if using *carbon tetrachloride.

Urine
Urine is acid, therefore sponge the stain with a mild *ammonia solution, or bicarbonate of soda and water to neutralize the acid. The stain can then be rinsed out in clean warm water. Wash in the usual way.

Vinegar

Mix 1 teaspoon *ammonia to 2 cups (½ liter) water and soak or sponge the article, and then leave it for a few minutes. Rinse well and wash as usual.

Water

Hold water-stained articles in the steam of a boiling kettle until the material is damp, shake frequently, then press with a warm iron. This is often enough to remove the stain.

Dip rayons, silks and delicate fabrics stained by sprinkled water in warm water. Gently squeeze out the excess water and roll in a towel, then iron while damp.

Rub rainwater spots with *denatured alcohol on a clean cloth.

Wax

Place blotting paper over the stain and press with a hot iron. Change the paper until all the grease has been absorbed. Use tissue paper and a cooler iron on silks and delicate fabrics.

Wine

Washable fabrics: Pour boiling water through the stain until it fades, or soak the article in a hot borax solution: 2 tablespoons (30 grams) to 2 cups (½ liter) water. Or rub the stain with lemon juice and salt. In all cases rinse well and wash as usual.

Sponge wool with *hydrogen peroxide solution, one part to six parts cold water. Then rinse well and wash as usual.

Nonwashable fabrics: Sponge the stain with the above borax solution, repeating several times, and rub dry with a clean cloth.

Rub colored fabrics with warm soapsuds or very weak *ammonia solution, then rub dry.

Odds and Ends
Odds and Ends
Odds and Ends
Odds and Ends
Odds and Ends
Odds and Ends
Odds and Ends
Odds and Ends
Odds and Ends
Odds and Ends
Odds and Ends
Odds and Ends
Odds and Ends
Odds and Ends
Odds and Ends

Baths

To clean enamel or porcelain baths, rub the sides with
*kerosene on a clean cloth. Then rinse well with hot water.

Brushes

To straighten bent bristles, hold them in the steam of a
boiling kettle, then remove from the steam and pull them
straight by hand. Repeat if necessary. Steam can cause
severe burns, so care must be taken.

Soak new bristle brushes with wooden heads in cold water
for about two hours to swell the wood and secure the
bristles. Then dry in a shaded place with the head of the
brush off the ground.

Wash all household bristle brushes in hot soapy water
with a little washing soda, then plunge them into cold
water and dry, head up, in the sun.

To clean hairbrushes, first remove the hair and dust, then
treat the back and handle according to the material. Wash
the bristles by beating them up and down in 1 qt. (1 liter)
warm soapy water with 1 teaspoon *ammonia added.
Rinse in warm, then cold water with a little salt to stiffen
the bristles. Then shake well and hang up to dry.

Cork

To clean cork mats, wash in cold water and rub with a
smooth pumice stone. Then rinse under cold running
water and dry in a cool place.

Curtain Hooks

Before use, rub curtain hooks with an oily rag. This
prevents rusting and helps to protect the curtains from
tearing.

To renovate old hooks, soak them in water with a little
*ammonia added. Then rinse in clean water and dry well.

Feathers

To clean decorative feathers, soak them in a basin of
*high-octane gasoline until they are clean, then dry
outside.

To clean white ostrich feathers, shred ½ cup (115 grams)
white soap and dissolve it in 2 qts. (2 liters) hot water in a
large basin. Beat the mixture into a lather, and soak the
feathers in it, rubbing them gently by hand until they are
clean. Then rinse in clean hot water. Shake well and hang
up to dry.

To prepare feathers for stuffing cushions, cut off the
downy tops and store them in paper bags until there are
enough to fill a cushion. Heat the bags in a moderate oven
for about half an hour. Check the oven frequently to
prevent the bags from catching fire.

Before stuffing the cushion, rub the ticking with beeswax
to stop the feathers from working through the material.

Keys and Zippers

To make stiff zippers and keys work smoothly, rub the
teeth with a lead pencil. This will last for months and is a
nongreasy lubricant.

Kneeling Pad

Fill an old hot-water bottle with chopped foam rubber to
make a very comfortable kneeling pad.

Odors

To get rid of the smell of new paint, place a handful of hay
in a bucket of warm water and leave in the room
overnight.

To prevent the smell of cabbage or cauliflower, add a little
lemon juice to the water while cooking.

Add lemon skins to the dishwater to eliminate the smell of

fish and onions from china and cutlery. It also softens the water and makes the china shine.

Pests

To catch fleas in beds, remove the bedclothes gently, and once the flea is found, dab it quickly with a piece of wet soap. This slows the flea down and makes it easier to catch.

Clusters of cloves hung up in a room will keep flies away.

To destroy cockroaches, mix equal parts of oatmeal with plaster of Paris and spread on the floor of the infested area. The cockroaches will eat this and die.

Pincushions

Sew a pincushion cover and fill it with dry coffee grounds. The needles and pins will not rust when stored in it.

Plants

To keep plants watered while away on vacation stand a bucket of water near the plants. Cut lengths of thick wool and place one end in the water and the other end into the plant pot. The wool will absorb the water and will drip onto the soil.

Rusty Irons

To clean a rusty iron, tie a piece of beeswax in a rag and rub the iron with the cloth when hot. Then scour the surface with a cloth sprinkled with salt. This will make the iron as clean and smooth as new. Keep the waxed cloth for further use.

Rusty Screws

To remove rusty screws that have become stuck, cover the head of the screw with *kerosene and leave it to soak in. Add more *kerosene if necessary.

Sponges and Loofahs

Soak sponges and loofahs when slimy in a strong solution of vinegar and water for twenty-four hours. Then rinse several times in cold water and dry outside.

Umbrellas

When new, grease the hinges well with petroleum jelly to prevent rusting.

To revive old silk umbrellas, dissolve 1 tablespoon sugar in 1 cup (¼ liter) boiling water. Open the umbrella and sponge the silk with the sugar solution, segment by segment, from the shaft out to the tips. Then hang the open umbrella on a line to dry.

Glossary

All the ingredients mentioned in this book are available from pharmacists, hardware stores, builders' merchants or art suppliers. They divide naturally into eight sections according to their functions. Some have several uses and may be found under a number of headings.

Please pay careful attention to the warnings on usage where they are given.

ABRASIVES

These are used for polishing or rubbing away other substances.

They vary in hardness and coarseness.

For polishing, use a comparatively coarse grade initially, gradually substituting finer grades.

Some abrasives have additives to aid in cleaning.

Emery Paper and Powder

This is a variety of mineral corundum in fine granular form, available in different grades. It is used for polishing metals and hard stones and for reconditioning furniture and smoothing chips in glass.

Pumice Powder

This is a porous volcanic stone containing silica. Many commercial scouring powders contain pumice.

Salt

It can be used as an abrasive. (See Alkalis)

Sandpaper

Sandpaper is available in different grades.

Steel Wool

Grade 000 is the finest grade of steel wool.

Whiting

This is a very finely powdered chalk used in cleaning
powders, polishes and in making putty. It is available
from art suppliers or painting and decorating stores.

ABSORBENTS

These are used for the removal of light, fresh or greasy
stains, by absorbing the staining substance which can then
be easily brushed away. They are harmless to all fabrics
but it is not recommended to use them on dark
nonwashable materials. They often work more effectively
if made into a paste with water before applying to the
stain.

Fuller's Earth

This is a hydrated compound of silica and alumina. It is
obtainable from a pharmacist.

Other Absorbents

Oatmeal, bran, salt, sand, stale bread crumbs, talcum
powder, starch, blotting paper, soft cloths, absorbent
cotton, paper napkins and tissues are all absorbents.

Tailor's Chalk

This is a soapstone or talc. It comes in solid or powdered
form.

ACIDS

Acids neutralize alkalis and will dissolve in water.

Acetic Acid and Vinegar

It can be used as a 10% solution to remove stains, but

more often white vinegar is used as it contains 5% acetic acid and is usually strong enough to deal with most stains.

Citric Acid

This is obtained from many fruit juices but especially from lemons. It can be bought in a pharmacy in diluted or powdered form, but lemon juice is equally as effective.

Oxalic Acid

This is obtained from the sorrel plant and is sold in crystal form in paint stores.

Commonly used in 5% solution, always adding the crystals to the water.

Do not use on synthetic fabrics.

*It is poisonous if swallowed. Avoid contact with skin or eyes.

ALKALIS

Alkalis neutralize acids and are soluble in water.

*Poisoning and burns from strong alkalis can be treated in an emergency by liberally applying vinegar or citric acid.

Ammonia

It is an alkaline gas dissolved in water and can be bought in varying strengths from pharmacies, groceries and hardware stores. Solutions of 5% to 15% are the most suitable. The chemical 10% pure solution is best for stain removal and cleaning.

*Ammonia is poisonous if swallowed. Store in a well-sealed container in a cool place out of the reach of children. Avoid contact with the skin or eyes.

*Never mix ammonia with any other cleaning agent as the combination could produce lethal gases.

Cloudy Ammonia

This is equally as caustic as ordinary ammonia and must be used with similar care.

It is a useful heavy household cleaner, excellent for scrubbing floors and bathroom cleaning.

To make cloudy ammonia, dissolve 2 oz. borax and 1 oz. powdered castile soap in 1 qt. hot water, then add 1 pint of ammonia and ¼ pint *denatured alcohol when the solution is cool. Add one or two tablespoons to 1 gallon water for use.

Common Table Salt

It is an excellent cleaner and stain remover.

Lye

This is a very strong alkali sold in crystal form.

*Always add the crystals to the water.

*Never add any other cleaning agents to caustic soda.

*It is extremely poisonous and inhaling the vapors should be avoided.

Avoid any contact with the skin or eyes as it can cause severe burning. If it does splash onto the skin, flood the burn with running water immediately.

Washing Sodas

An effective cleaner sold in crystal form.

It is very soluble in water and acts as a water softener.

EMULSIFIERS

These are substances that mix with grease or resinous particles and hold them in suspension making them easy to remove or dissolve.

Ammonia and washing soda are both emulsifiers (see above).

Soap

Soaps are known as built or unbuilt.

Unbuilt soaps contain a high proportion of pure soap with a little moisture and salt. They are expensive and very mild, suitable for toiletries and laundering fine fabrics.

Built soaps contain additives like borax, alkaline water softeners and washing soda, etc., which help in removing heavily soiled cloths. They are very effective in hard water.

Synthetic Detergents

They have good wetting and penetrating properties and are more easily rinsed out of fabrics than soap.

SOLVENTS

These are substances which, when applied, mix with and dissolve the material to be removed. There are many types of solvents so it is important to analyze the stain to be removed and select the correct solvent.

Acetone

*This is a highly inflammable colorless liquid, with a heavy toxic peppermint smell. Avoid breathing the fumes or contact with the eyes. Only use in a well-ventilated place. Do not use near naked flames. Store in a well-sealed container in a cool place, out of reach of children.

It is harmless to natural fibers but will damage synthetic materials, including acetates.

Kerosene will counteract the action of acetone.

Amyl Acetate

*This is a chemical compound of acetic acid and amyl

alcohol with a heavy toxic smell. Avoid breathing the vapor or contact with eyes, and always use in a well-ventilated place. It is also highly inflammable, so avoid using near naked flames. It is also poisonous if taken internally.

Carbon Tetrachloride
*This is a clear nonflammable liquid which evaporates very rapidly, giving off a heavy toxic vapor. Avoid breathing the fumes and contact with the eyes. Always use in a well-ventilated place.

Denatured Alcohol
*This is poisonous, highly inflammable with a strong noxious vapor. Care must be taken during use. Only use in a well-ventilated space, away from any naked flames. Store in a well-sealed container in a cool place out of reach of children.

It is safe to use on most fabrics and evaporates quickly.

Ethyl Acetate
*This acts in a similar way to amyl acetate, and has the same heavy toxic fumes and is highly inflammable.

Ethyl Alcohol
This is the main alcoholic content of wines, beers and liquors. Gin is useful for cleaning certain stones in jewelry.

Gasoline
*This is a hydrocarbon mixture distilled from petroleum, which evaporates at normal temperatures. In liquid form it is highly inflammable, but if confined in a container with air, it will explode violently when in contact with fire. Use with great care, well away from naked flames. Avoid breathing the fumes or contact with the eyes, and use in a well-ventilated place.

Never use it to clean silk as the rubbing friction can cause a spark which could explode the vapor.

Kerosene
*This is obtained by distilling crude gasoline and is highly inflammable and must not be used near a naked flame.

Lighter Fluid
*This is a super-refined gasoline with all the properties of ordinary gas, so the same precautions apply.

Rubbing Alcohol
This is a powerful disinfectant. It is much weaker than *denatured alcohol.

Turpentine
*This is a resinous juice obtained from pine and fir trees and is highly inflammable and poisonous. Avoid using near naked flames and breathing the vapor. Always use in a well-ventilated place.

Water
Water and steam dissolve water-based glues, sugary substances and salts.

BLEACHES
Bleaches are chemical agents used to whiten materials, especially white fabrics, and to remove certain stains.

Always follow the instructions on the container and use with care.

*They weaken fabrics and fade colors if not used properly.

*Do not store in metal containers.

Citric Acid and Vinegar
Both these have mild bleaching powers.

Chlorine Bleach

This is ordinary household bleach.

*Do not use on wool, silk, leather or resin-coated cotton, linen and rayon fabrics that are already weak.

Always test on an unimportant area of fabric before using, and rinse very thoroughly after use.

Do not add bleach to water containing clothes.

*Never mix chlorine bleach with any other cleaning agents like ammonia, etc., as they mix to give off dangerous toxic fumes.

Hydrogen Peroxide

This is a good bleach, safe to use on all fabrics. It is available from the pharmacy as 20 volume strength and use it diluted; 1 part to 6 parts cold water.

*Always pour down the drain once used, and store in a cool dark place away from children.

Sodium Perborate Bleach

This is not as strong as chlorine bleach and is safe to use on all fabrics.

It is obtainable from the pharmacy in crystal form.

*Do not store in metal containers.

OILS

These lubricate dried leather and soften certain stains to make removal easier.

Castor Oil

It is obtained from the bean of the castor oil plant. It is a good leather conditioner and is particularly effective on leathers that need to be polished.

Lanolin

This is obtained from the natural grease of wool. It is a lubricant.

Linseed Oil

This originates from the flax plant, used for making varnishes, paints and many furniture polishes.

When buying, specify whether "raw" or "boiled" linseed oil is wanted.

For recipes which recommend boiled linseed oil, this does not mean that it is necessary to boil the oil, but is a special process that can be done only by experts.

Petroleum Jelly

It is a soft greasy substance obtained from petroleum.

Index